Nature's Wrath

Erica Varney

Illustrations by Derrick Wiliams

1   2   3   4   5   6   7   8   9   10

ISBN 0-8250-4974-6

Copyright © 2004

Walch Publishing

P. O. Box 658 • Portland, Maine 04104-0658

walch.com

Printed in the United States of America

Nature's Wrath

Table of Contents

Nature's Wrath

Introduction

Disasters happen when you least expect them. You may hear about earthquakes or tornadoes on the news. Then you probably think, *That won't happen to me.* You might be right. But you could also be wrong.

What we know about disasters comes from two sources. Scientists explain why they happen. But we can also learn from the people who have experienced them. The stories in this book come from both scientists and eyewitnesses. Survivors lived to tell of their experiences. That's what makes these stories so interesting.

Many of these disasters happened a long

time ago. But that doesn't mean that they won't happen again. Technology helps scientists to predict some disasters. You may have more of a warning than victims did years ago. But the power of the disaster could be even greater.

Years from now you could be telling your grandchildren about your escape from nature's wrath. That's just what the people in these stories did.

Mount Vesuvius

Would you ever live on a volcano? Ancient Romans did. In fact, they did not worry about it. They had no idea that it would erupt. The soil at the foot of the mountain was rich. It was perfect for gardens and vineyards. People settled the area without a second thought.

Mount Vesuvius is located in Italy near the Bay of Naples. It was created on the northern side of a seismic fault between Europe and Africa. Before 79 C.E. (Common Era), it was near two Roman cities—Pompeii and Herculaneum. But these two cities no longer exist. They vanished in one of the volcano's most famous eruptions. It wasn't until another eruption centuries later that the cities were found.

Mount Vesuvius

How do we know so much about a volcano that erupted so many years ago? A young man named Pliny the Younger wrote an account of the event. He wrote what he saw in a letter to a historian. His uncle, Pliny the Elder, commanded a fleet of war ships. He used his ships to get closer to the volcano. He wanted to see the amazing sight up close. And he wanted to rescue those in need.

In the year 79 C.E., Pliny the Younger's mother saw an unusual cloud. She called for the elder Pliny to look at it. Pliny the Younger described the cloud as looking like "a pine tree, for it shot up to a great height in the form of a very tall trunk, which spread itself out at the top into a sort of branches." Some miles away, the volcano had erupted.

On August 24, the land around Mount Vesuvius shook with tremors of an earthquake. Around 1 P.M. the top of the mountain split open. A giant cloud poured out. "Sometimes it [the cloud] looked white, sometimes blotched and dirty, according to the amount of soil and ashes it carried with it." The cloud of ash and pumice—a kind of volcanic rock—shot up into the sky 12 to 20 miles. It was the middle of the day. But it was as dark as night. Those who lived in Pompeii were covered with ash, stones, and pumice.

Within one hour, 6 inches of debris blanketed the city. The volcano hurled hot debris into the air for almost eight hours.

Pliny the Elder approached the volcano with his fleet of ships. Hot cinders fell on the decks. As the ships got closer, the rocks and cinders got hotter. He ordered the ships to stop. He thought about turning back. But he decided against it. His curiosity pushed him on.

When they reached land, the sailors did not know where to go. They could go to the houses, which were shaking. Or they could go to open fields, which were being showered with hot stones and

cinders. The brave men tied pillows on their heads with napkins. They headed for the fields with their heads covered. Even though it was daytime, the sky was dark. The men used torches.

Pliny the Elder was having trouble breathing. This was not unusual for him. But the gases in the air made it even worse. He rested on a cloth. Then he called for some water to drink. When he got up to drink it, he fell dead.

Pliny's men lived. They made it back to his nephew. They told him about their travels. Because of Pliny the Elder's effort, we know much more about the eruption of Mount Vesuvius.

Pliny the Younger wrote what his uncle saw and what he himself saw. He and his mother stayed together during the eruption. One of his most vivid descriptions is of the sounds he heard. "You might hear the shrieks of women, the screams of children, and the shouts of men; some calling for their children, others for their parents, others for their husbands, and seeking to recognize each other by the voices that replied." He later wrote that some people just wished to die. Others prayed to the gods.

At first, Herculaneum wasn't hit that hard. It was upwind of the volcano. So it was just covered with a light coating of ash. But around midnight, part of the volcano collapsed. This sent an avalanche of hot debris down the mountain. Herculaneum was buried under a river of mud. It was 65 feet deep in places! The city was sealed away as if it had never existed.

Some people of Pompeii and Herculaneum were able to escape the falling debris. When the eruption finally ended, those from Pompeii were able to go back. They could find some of their belongings. But their homes were ruined. The survivors of Herculaneum suffered a total loss. With all the mud that covered the city, they were lucky to have escaped at all. More than 3,300 people died within two days.

When volcanoes erupt, their appearances change. Mount Vesuvius didn't look the same at all. Before the eruption, it had been flat on the top. Now there was a large cone on the top. The cone was made up of ashes, cinders, and stones that were thrown up during the eruption. The forests, gardens, and vineyards that once covered the slopes of the volcano were gone.

For centuries no one knew about the two buried cities. In 1713, a man was digging a well. He found the remains of Herculaneum—24 feet underground! No one paid much attention at the time. But in 1748, someone found ancient works of art while digging in a vineyard. Twelve feet below the surface, the remains of Pompeii were found. Because mud had sealed Herculaneum, more of its remains were uncovered.

People have been digging in these two lost cities since then. Entire skeletons have been found. One skeleton was uncovered with a chain around one leg. This was probably a slave trying to flee from his master.

Mount Vesuvius is currently the only active volcano in Europe. It has erupted many times since 79 C.E. The last known eruption took place in 1944, during World War II when Allied forces were attacking Italy.

People who study volcanoes expect that Vesuvius' next eruption will be destructive. With today's technology, however, it is safe to live on Mount Vesuvius. Over two million people live near the volcano. The people who live at the base of the volcano will have some warning before it erupts again. They will have time to leave. Their property will be lost or damaged. But their lives will be spared.

The smell of spring filled the New York City air. People were excited about an early spring in 1888. Temperatures reached into the upper 50s in March. On Sunday, March 11, 1888, rain poured through the mild air. People went to bed that evening thinking they would wake up to a balmy spring morning. But they woke up to the opposite.

In 1888, the science of weather forecasting was not very advanced. No one knew that two storms were combining on the east coast to make a giant storm. One storm came from the south, and one came from the north. As the storms moved, the winds shifted. This mixed warm air with cold air. The result was an unexpected monster.

The Blizzard of 1888

They called it the "Great White Hurricane." In the early hours of Monday morning, the rain changed to hail, to sleet, and then to snow. The temperature dropped to single digits. Winds howled through the city. By 7 A.M., 10 inches of snow covered the ground. New Yorkers woke up to the blizzard of a lifetime.

Snow swirled through the air. People could barely see through the whitewash. One man wrote, "The air looked as though some people were throwing buckets full of flour from all the rooftops—the snow was so thick and of such smallness of flakes." The whistling winds blew the snow into drifts up to 5 feet high. On some streets, the snow was piled high on one side. On the other side, the sidewalks were bare. First-floor windows and doors were buried. One woman remembered, "If you wanted to look out into the street, you had to go to the second floor."

Eveything was caked with snow. "The trees no longer looked like trees; they looked like ghostly, white giants bending under a crushing burden."

Today we can turn on the television or the radio to get the weather forecast. We can find out what events have been canceled before we leave the house. In 1888, this was not so. Many people left

The Blizzard of 1888

for work that morning,
unaware of the risky
conditions. Outside,
they found themselves

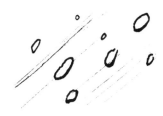

braving wind gusts of up to 48 miles per
hour.

The morning commute had begun. But
many never reached their destinations.
People were trapped on trains that ran
above the street. The trains had derailed.
What they thought would be a short train
ride turned into hours in a frigid train car.
Men blew on their cupped hands to keep
them warm. One man recalled that "most
of the passengers were walking up and
down the cars to maintain their

circulation." Fire ladders were later raised up to the trains to help the people escape.

Some weren't lucky enough to be on a train that sheltered them. They braved the streets on foot. One woman recalled seeing "a man trying to cross 96th Street for an hour and a half. We watched him start, get a quarter of the way across and then get flung back against the building on the corner. The last time he tried it, he was caught up in a whirl of snow and disappeared from our view." People caught outside tried to find shelter. Hotels, coffee shops, and bars flooded with people. Cabs—horse-drawn carriages— were scarce. The drivers charged high prices to work their horses so hard. Many routes were blocked by snowdrifts. One survivor said that "the drifts of snow were up to the horses' shoulders."

Utility poles buckled under the pressure of the snow. Some were torn down by falling trees. In the evening, the only lights were from candles and gas lights. Telephone and telegraph wires lay on the ground. Service was knocked out for days. The postal service was shut down, too. New York City was isolated from the outside world.

The poor suffered immensely. In 1888, people used coal to heat their homes. The price of coal went up so much during the storm that the poor could not afford to heat their homes. They had to look for ways to make money fast. They shoveled snow. They helped stranded people and charged for it. Wealthier people could rely on their stocked items throughout the storm. But the poor lived day to day. They didn't have food and coal stored in their homes.

Despite the bitter cold and massive amounts of snow, New Yorkers stayed in good spirits. They were helpful to those in need. And they didn't lose their sense of humor. One woman remembered seeing signs "in various places, stuck into the

snowdrifts" reading "Keep off the grass."
"Do not pick any flowers." "Important
notice: This is 23rd Street."

The blizzard continued for 36 hours.
After the first day, it grew even colder.
The whirling snow and slush became ice.
School was closed for a week. About 200
people died in the storm. They froze,
starved, or died from exhaustion. By the
end of the storm, almost two feet of snow
had fallen.

When the blizzard finally ended, New
Yorkers faced the cleanup. Some lit fires
in the snow banks to melt the snow. Most
cleared the snow by shoveling it by hand.

They then carted it to the Hudson River. Twelve million loads of snow were dumped into the river. As the snow was removed, frozen bodies of people and animals were uncovered. In shady areas, piles of snow didn't fully melt until June.

The Blizzard of 1888 changed New York City forever. It led to the burial of wires underground and to the creation of the subway system. With today's technology, a storm of this size would not be as harmful—or would it?

The Johnstown Flood

Imagine a time bomb just waiting to go off. Imagine *knowing the time bomb was there*—and not doing anything about it.

The Johnstown Flood

This is what the people of Johnstown, Pennsylvania, did in the late 1800s. Their time bomb was a dam that held water in a lake. It was only a matter of time before the dam burst.

Floods were a way of life in Johnstown. They happened every year. The town had been built on a flat area between mountains. It is located at the fork of the Little Conemaugh and Stony Creek rivers. Each year after heavy rains or rapid melting of snow, water from the rivers would fill the streets. People would move their belongings to the second floor of their homes. There was not much else they could do. When the streets were flooded in 1889, they did not think much of it.

Fourteen miles away from the town, the South Fork Dam held up Lake Conemaugh on the side of a mountain. This lake was 450 feet higher than the town. It was owned by the South Fork Fishing and Hunting Club. The wealthy members of the club stocked the lake with fish. They made the area into a beautiful resort. But they failed to take care of the dam. They removed pipes and put in screens to keep the fish from escaping. This made it hard to control the lake's level. This was a recipe for disaster.

The Johnstown Flood

On May 30, 1889, heavy rains flooded the rivers. They filled the lake. They flowed through the streets. Between 6 and 10 inches fell over 24 hours. This was just another rainy season in Johnstown.

By the morning of May 31, Lake Conemaugh had risen over 2 feet. Men dashed to repair the dam, but it was no use. Telegraph lines and railroad tracks were washed out. The water rose an inch every ten minutes. By 10 A.M., the water was less than a foot from the top of the dam. A courier was sent on horseback to warn the 30,000 people of Johnstown. He rode through the streets shouting, "Run to the hills, the reservoir is breaking!"

People started to flee, but it was too late. The dam could not hold. At 3:15 P.M., the dam made of earth, rock, and clay finally gave way.

Within 45 minutes, the lake that once held 20 million tons of water was empty. Moving at 40 miles per hour, the "rolling ball" of water picked up everything in its path. It grew with every inch it moved. Witnesses said that the height of the water reached 40 feet. This was as high as a three-story building! With hills on either side of the water, it had nowhere else to go. The rolling mass was half a mile wide.

By 4:07 P.M., the giant mass of water

rolled into Johnstown. What started as a distant rumble became a violent "roar like thunder." It plowed through the town with such force that it picked up houses. It carried away mills, railroad cars, livestock, pets, and people. One survivor recalled seeing "no water, just an immense wall of rubbish, dark and squirming with rooftops, huge roots, and planks." People were swept up in muddy water with debris all around them. Some were caught in barbed wire that had come from the wire factory. The wreckage was grinding together. This crushed many people. Others were saved by the debris. They used floating objects as rafts. Another survivor remembered that "a large roof came floating toward me with about 20 people on it. I cried and called across the water to them to help me . . . they were holding on for dear life, feeling every minute that they would be tossed to death." Within 10 minutes, the whole town was ruined.

The debris smacked into Pennsylvania Railroad's stone bridge. The water flowed through the arches. But the objects it had picked up got caught there. The debris saved many people. It blocked them from getting past the bridge. But others were not so lucky. They were left to drown in the rushing water. Some were able to escape the floating waste that had saved them. Others were still holding on when a mass of objects caught fire. Just when they thought they were saved, 80 people burned to death. The fire may have started from some house's coal stove.

Darkness came while people struggled for their lives. Some were still on top of floating debris. Families huddled in the attics of the few intact homes. Relief came, but it took a long time. It was hard to spread word of the disaster. And it was almost impossible for anyone to get into the town. When relief finally did arrive, it came from all over. Supplies and money came from all 50 states and from other countries.

Over 2,200 people lost their lives to the flood. Many of them were never found. Some bodies were found hundreds of miles away. Relief workers placed the bodies in pine boxes. They wrote descriptions of the people inside and taped these to the boxes. Then they waited for families to come identify them. Some were never identified. Their whole families had died. One out of three bodies remained unclaimed.

The members of the South Fork

Fishing and Hunting Club were blamed for the flood. They failed to maintain the dam. But because floods happened all the time in this area, the club was never formally charged. If the dam had been taken care of, would it have been enough to hold all the water? No one knows for sure.

1906 San Francisco Earthquake

April 18, 1906, dawned clear and bright. Most of San Francisco, California, was still fast asleep. The early risers were just getting up. Children were not yet out of bed to get ready for school. Those who were still in bed were in for the most powerful alarm of their lives.

At 5:12 A.M., a foreshock rumbled through the city. In 20 to 25 seconds, vibrations shook the city. People were thrown out of bed. Parents dashed to find their young children. The whole city held on for dear life. Pictures fell from walls. Pianos and beds slid across rooms. Dishes crashed to the floor. Chimneys crumbled to the ground. One survivor remembered it growing "constantly worse, the noise deafening . . . made such a roar that no one noise could be distinguished." On that morning, San Francisco was rocked by an earthquake.

An earthquake cannot be predicted. The city of San Francisco lies on a giant crack, or fault. This crack is called the San Andreas Fault. The fault is made up of two separate pieces of earth, called tectonic plates. When these plates move, they rub against each other. The plates are huge, irregular pieces of rock. They are not smooth. When they move, rocks break off and create vibrations. These vibrations are what cause havoc on the Earth's surface.

The quake caused just as much chaos

above the earth's crust. Power and trolley lines snapped in half. Electric wires lay on the ground. Bricks and glass showered the city streets. Buildings collapsed. One eyewitness remembers that "the air was filled with falling stones. People around me were crushed to death on all sides. All around the huge buildings were shaking and waving . . . I thought the end of the world had come." In places the streets had sunk three or four feet. In other places, the streets were humped up four or five feet high.

The earthquake went on for 45 to 60 seconds. Those who survived say that one minute felt a lot longer. The quake rocked

1906 San Francisco Earthquake

San Francisco the hardest. But it was felt as far away as Los Angeles, Oregon, and Nevada. Along the fault, 290 miles of the earth's surface was cracked open. Trees along the fault were uprooted or snapped in half.

Although the earthquake lasted only a matter of seconds, the ruin went on for days. The worst damage was caused by fire. During the quake, gas lines burst and stoves fell over. This led to a giant blaze.

The fires spread. And there was little that anyone could do to put them out. Most of the water mains had broken during the quake. Water was very scarce. One man was crushed beneath burning wreckage. He begged a policeman to kill him. When the fire spread to the man's feet, the officer wrote down his name and shot him in the head.

The streets swarmed with people. Families ran for safety. People saved as many of their belongings as they could. One man recalled people packing up their things: "Some people used sewing machines and piled stuff on them, then rolled them along the walks. Others were dragging trunks, lugging parrots in cages, and dogs and cats and monkeys on strings." They all headed for the bay. Water meant safety. Getting out of the city meant safety. People needed to be in the open where buildings would not crush them. Leaving on boats or on the ferry was the answer.

It did not take long to organize help. Very early on, the fire chief was crushed to death under a hotel. But that did not stop the firemen and rescue workers. They began pumping water from the bay. But the fires were too far away for the hoses to reach. One survivor said that "the heat became so intense no one could get close enough to do any good. The water just went up in steam and they had to give up." Another answer was needed. They used dynamite to blow up buildings. Once the buildings were gone, there was nothing to go up in flames. One man later wrote, "I saw some of the finest and most beautiful buildings in the city, new modern palaces, blown to atoms." The dynamite worked. But it took days to put out all the flames.

Those left in the city were forced to set up camp in public parks away from the fires. The military provided tents, food, and clothing. Water was another story. One woman recalled, "Water was now more precious than gold, and not a drop must be wasted." At night the fires made a vivid glow. Lights were not needed, even though the flames were miles away. When the wind blew, ashes showered over the people. Smoke stung their eyes. But despite their losses, the people were full of hope. One woman described everyone as "all so good-natured and ready for a smile! I never saw one person crying."

Over half the people of San Francisco were left homeless. Almost 30,000 buildings were lost. Anywhere from 700 to 3,000 people died. The Great Quake led to a lot of research. Since then, houses have been built to be earthquake-safe. But even earthquake-safe homes can be destroyed. Just ask the survivors of the 1989 San Francisco Earthquake.

They were stranded. They had been
stranded for days. The passengers of a
Great Northern Railway train were headed

The Wellington Avalanche

to Seattle from Spokane, Washington. When they boarded the train on February 23, 1910, they had no idea how long they would be on it. And they had no idea of the disaster that was to come.

Imagine being trapped on an airplane for days. The plane is grounded because of poor weather. Just when the runway clears and the plane takes off, it has to land again because of more bad weather. This is what happened to the train headed to Seattle. The train was halted just before a two-mile tunnel because of snow slides. Two days later, the tracks were cleared. The train forged through the tunnel—only to be stranded on the other side. This was near the small town of Wellington. From Thursday night to Tuesday, the train sat in the same spot.

The passengers grew restless and hungry. They were only allowed two meals a day. Some hiked eight miles to the next town. Others trekked through the endless snow to a railroad cook shack for breakfast. After three days in the same spot, the passengers wanted to move. They did not think they were safe. Snow slides were rushing by them. They wanted to move back into the tunnel. Superintendent James O'Neill assured them they were safe. Avalanches had never occurred in the spot where they were resting.

The snow kept falling. It fell at a rate of one foot per hour. There had never been so much snow in the mountains before. On Monday, the snow changed to sleet and then to rain—the perfect conditions for an avalanche.

An avalanche happens when a layer of snow loses its grip on a slope and then slides downhill. Picture a mass of wet snow that thaws and slides off a roof. Avalanches can be triggered by several things. They include earthquake tremors, human error, or heavy rainfall. In this case, it was rain.

The Wellington Avalanche

The temperature began to rise. When warm air meets cold air, thunderstorms usually occur. In the early hours of March 1, a thunder and lightning storm rocked the small town of Wellington. As one survivor recalled, "Lightning flashes were vivid and a tearing wind was howling down the canyon. Suddenly there was a dull roar." The rain and high winds caused an ice shelf to break loose hundreds of feet above the railroad tracks. Snow, slush, and ice hurtled downhill. It picked up everything in its path. It grew to be a quarter of a mile wide.

Avalanches are common, but they do not always hurt people. Sometimes only trees and boulders are in their way. But in this case, the train was in the wrong place at the wrong time. The avalanche threw the train off its tracks, along with another mail train nearby. The trains tumbled down the mountain in the mass of snow and other debris. A train employee, far away from the trains at the time, heard a rumble. He later described what he saw: "It picked up cars and equipment as though they were so many snow-draped toys, and swallowing them up, disappeared like a white, broad monster into the ravine below."

The people who had hiked to town were lucky. Those who stayed on the train were not. When the avalanche plowed through the trains, it took 122 people with it. The train cars were swept up along with trees and boulders. After plummeting down the hill 150 feet, they were buried in wreckage. Over 40 feet of snow and debris covered the victims.

The Wellington Avalanche

Imagine being buried alive in freezing snow and debris! The snow was heavy with rainwater. Some of the victims were closer to the top of the wreckage. They struggled to break free. Some escaped and helped others. But it was dark. The only light they had was of lightning from the storm.

More help was on the way, but it took six hours for help to arrive. It seemed to take forever. People arrived with shovels and started to dig. By the time they reached the victims, most were just dead bodies. They were packed in the snow as if it were cement. Rescue workers risked their lives to help the victims. More avalanches were possible. Doctors and nurses hiked to the scene. They set up a field hospital in a shed in town.

The rescuers did not have coffins. They had to wrap the bodies in blankets. They used sleds to carry the dead away. It took weeks to find all the bodies. One was not uncovered until June. Some bodies ended up in the stream at the bottom of the mountain. They floated away and were never found. Twenty-two people survived. But 96 people perished. Thirty-five of them were passengers. The rest were railroad employees.

The town is no longer named

The Wellington Avalanche

Wellington. The name became linked with the disaster, so it was changed to Tye. Several avalanches occur each year in Washington state. In 1910, one of them was a killer.

The Tri-State Tornado

The weather forecast called for rain and strong shifting winds. It did not call for the worst tornado in history.

The Tri-State Tornado

People first spotted the Tri-State Tornado in Ellington, Missouri, just after 1:00 P.M., on March 25, 1925. Trees began to snap in half. A farmer was killed. The storm grew into a giant and whisked across Missouri. One schoolgirl remembers, "The walls seemed to fall in, all around us. Then the floor at one end of the building gave way. We all slipped or slid in that direction. . . . Children all around me were cut and bleeding. They screamed and cried. . . . I had to close my eyes."

Eleven people perished in Missouri. The tornado smashed most of the town of Annapolis. Survivors recall the storm as being so big and so low to the ground that no one could tell it was a tornado. The twister sucked up everything it touched. As one survivor recalls, "The air was filled with 10,000 things. Boards, poles, cans, garments, stoves, whole sides of the little frame houses, in some cases the houses themselves, were picked up and smashed to earth. . . . A baby was blown from its mother's arms. A cow . . . was hurled into the village restaurant."

The monster tornado then crossed the border into southern Illinois. Gorham was hit around 2:30. Thirty-four people died without even knowing what had hit them. Over half the town lay wounded in the

tornado's path. The cyclone
was now at the height of its destruction.
More lives were lost—234—in
Murphysboro than in any other U.S. city
at that time. In about 40 minutes, the Tri-
State Tornado had killed 541 people.

Plowing through DeSoto, Illinois, the
great funnel wiped out an entire school. In
the mining town of West Frankfort,
Illinois, about 800 miners were working

500 feet below the ground. They didn't know there was a storm until they lost electrical power. Being so far underground saved them from the violence of the twister. When they climbed out of the mine, many found wives and children dead or hurt. Their homes were in ruins. If only their families could have been down in the mines with them!

The cyclone blasted into Indiana as children were getting out of school for the day. Many never made it home. Most of the students who survived no longer had houses to go home to. The town of Griffin was the worst hit town in the state. Almost 150 homes were ruined. The tornado then plowed through the town of Princeton. Many farms were lost in that area. The massive tornado finally let up about 10 miles northeast of Princeton. It had killed at least 71 people in Indiana.

The Tri-State Tornado was the worst storm people had ever seen. It broke many records. Some of these records have still not been broken, over 75 years later. At three and a half hours, it is the longest-running tornado ever recorded. The storm moved at an average speed of 62 miles per hour—as fast as many cars travel on the highway. At some points the tornado moved even faster than that. The wind speeds inside the funnel cloud reached up to 300 miles per hour. The most surprising number is the 695 people who perished. This is the most people a single tornado has ever killed. Over 2,000 people were injured. In the three states, 15,000 homes were destroyed. Many of them were never rebuilt.

The Tri-State Tornado was truly amazing. So were the people who survived. Larger homes made it through the storm. The owners gave food, shelter, and clothing to those who had none. Army soldiers set up what they called "tent cities." People who had lost their homes stayed in these tents. Supplies came in trains and trucks. Food, clothes, money, and medical supplies arrived in the devastated area. Caskets were even sent to the towns. The American Red Cross also helped. A St. Louis newspaper described the picture: "Scenes of suffering and horror marked the storm and fire. Throughout the night, relief workers and ambulances endeavored to make their way through the streets strewn with wreckage, fallen telegraph poles and wires and burning embers. The only light afforded was that of the burning area."

Unlike in 1925, today we have tornado warning systems in place. We can find out about tornados and other storms on the radio and on television. We now have more time to prepare for these monstrous storms. Even though we can predict bad weather, however, we cannot control it. People are still at the mercy of nature.